The Art
of
Egg Decorating

The Art
of
Egg Decorating

Allan Stacey

Routledge & Kegan Paul
London, Boston and Henley

First published in 1982
by Routledge & Kegan Paul Ltd
39 Store Street, London WC1E 7DD,
9 Park Street, Boston, Mass. 02108, USA and
Broadway House, Newtown Road, Henley-on-Thames, Oxon RG9 1EN
Set by
Rowland Phototypesetting Ltd, Bury St Edmunds, Suffolk
and printed in Great Britain by
St Edmundsbury Press, Bury St Edmunds, Suffolk

Library of Congress Cataloguing in Publication Data

Stacey, Allan, 1928-
The art of egg decorating.
Includes index.
1. Egg decoration.   I. Title.
TT896.7.S7   745.594'4   81-17697

ISBN 0-7100-9026-9 AACR2

For birds everywhere,
without whom this craft
would not be possible

Contents

Preface

Many years ago I became interested in the egg-shape and its decorative possibilities. I began by painting eggs with water colours. After a time I found that oil or acrylic paints were better to handle and latterly I have used only acrylic paints for creating, say, a panel or group of flowers.

The eggs I have worked on are those laid by either geese or turkeys and decoration is a lengthy process. The cutting, hardening, hingeing, lining and mounting all take a great deal of time. One needs to be extremely patient and careful and one also needs to possess an Olympian ability to hold one's breath!

I spend about thirty hours making the more complicated eggs and even more time if there is a musical movement involved. Each of my musical eggs has a different hidden mechanism to start the tune playing. This secret becomes the owner's. Some also have a secret drawer hidden inside, or have other surprises.

I have been collecting materials for some years and would mention here how grateful I am to family and friends who have given me many relics from the past. Apart from Britain, my materials come from far-flung places. From India I have bought topaz and garnets and Kashmiri lapis and in Europe and especially Italy I have discovered all manner of jewellery and 'findings'.

Each egg I have made has had incorporated into the design a piece of antique jewellery or a relic from the past, and this makes it unique. Wherever I travel I look out for a likely piece of metal, silver or porcelain that I can one day put to good use. Two baroque key handles made of ormolu have made beautiful finials for the tops of eggs; these I found in Venice.

To anyone with imagination, determination and time, the decoration of eggs is a fascinating pursuit. Whether one boils them in onion skins at Eastertime or decorates them with diamonds and pearls, the results are sure to be satisfying.

This book gives information and instructions on the craft of egg decorating within the author's experience.

There are as many alternatives as there are eggs and decorators, and it is acknowledged that many methods and materials are not included.

I hope this book will encourage many to take up this rewarding hobby.

1
The egg as a symbol

The custom of decorating eggs is very old and the craft has many associations. The ancient Druids, for instance, considered eggs sacred and forbade the eating of them and some of the Druids wore the 'egg-shape' round their necks, inlaid with gold and this was symbolic of rank.

From pagan times the egg, either as a symbol of birth, fertility or rebirth, has remained an indestructible symbol of goodness. The egg, having retained its shape throughout the centuries, seems to underline its perfection of form and to suggest a needlessness of evolutionary change.

Pagans, Christians, Jews, Muslims, Hindus, Greeks, in fact all peoples either religiously or superstitiously have, throughout the ages, believed that the egg possesses mystic or magical powers.

The egg is symbolic of life and as such the egg-shape has proven timelessly attractive. Until the egg is cracked open life is beyond the sight of man, hidden in a 'case' so fragile that the slightest knock would reveal the mystery within. This very fragility must have gained great respect for eggs, especially the egg-shape, and the many ways that people have decorated egg-shells over the centuries underlines their constant fascination for so many different nationalities.

In the main it is the women who handle eggs, in the course of cooking, and it is they who have invented and perpetuated the many methods of decorating the egg-shell and have passed their art down through the years, through their children, especially at festival times.

Though not exclusively an Easter custom, it is nevertheless this time of the year, when families are celebrating the festival of Resurrection, the continuance of life after death, that has provoked the most inspiration for decorating egg-shells.

The egg-shells may be painted or dyed or jewelled and to give and to exchange them would, to many, be symbolic of everlasting life. To others it would just be a wish of good luck or a token of love or of esteem.

It is doubtful if the present-day giving of eggs at Easter time, especially the chocolate ones, has any deeper significance than a chance to say Happy Easter, though this custom is valuable in that it does continue the giving of eggs.

I have often thought that it would be more appropriate to give eggs at Christmas time, it being a more carefree and jovial time of the year, celebrating as it does the birth of Christ. I suppose rebirth *after* death is more mysterious than just birth, which is happening all the time.

I once lived in Lancashire, near the scene of the setting for Harrison Ainsworth's *The Lancashire Witches*, and at Eastertime we children would write our names on hard-boiled hen's eggs and would then take them to a place called Whalley Nab. This was a steep hill-scape, fissured by ravines, and there we would roll our eggs down the grass slopes. There was great competition as to whose eggs would roll furthest and should the eggs of a boy and a girl crash together at the bottom it was said that they would marry each other one day!

The best time for egg rolling was when Easter fell early. Then the grasses and tufts of budding ferns were still dormant, making the way easier for the eggs to roll freely. When Easter was late and grass and ferns and flowers were well developed the eggs had to be helped down-hill with sticks and egg rolling became more like hazardous hockey.

This egg rolling at Easter time is practised in many European countries and in many counties in Britain, though in Britain it seems to be seen more in the northern parts.

The practice of decorating egg-shells, though, does continue all over Britain and Europe and throughout the Commonwealth and there is a great deal of interest in the art in America. In fact all over the world the 'art form', or craft, is becoming popular.

Egg-decorating customs differ from country to country and where, in one place, the egg will be comparatively plain, in another it will be covered with intricate decoration that will have taken many hours to achieve. An example of this can be seen by comparing a Greek egg which has been dipped in red dye, perhaps revealing the outline of a pressed flower which had been stuck to it, with one of the Moravian batik-designed eggs, whose patterns are geometric fantasies, each differing in some minute detail of colour or of pattern.

These beautiful multi-coloured Moravian eggs, as well as similar ones from such places as Slovakia, Austria, Germany, Bohemia, Romania, Poland or the Ukraine, cannot, though, outshine the Imperial eggs made by Peter Carl Fabergé for the Russian royal family.

Comparing any other decorated eggs with those made by Fabergé is unfair as the materials used by Fabergé were not only very different from the real egg-shell, which by its fragility sets limits upon possible design, but Fabergé used gold and silver and ormulu, and real stones. His eggs are unique.

In an age of opulence, when Fabergé was creating his beautiful eggs, it is surprising that no other court, European or otherwise, provided patronage which encouraged craftsmen to make decorated eggs. Only the name of Fabergé seems to be associated with those eggs which are richly decorated with precious stones or inlaid with fine enamels and elaborately constructed from precious metals.

There are records of eggs being decorated as far back as the thirteenth century. Religious themes were most common, especially connected with folk art; then the egg featured as a symbol of life or as a wish for a good life. Gold-leafed eggs were exchanged as talismans of good fortune by members of the court of Edward I.

Later, in the sixteenth century, Francis I of France was presented with an egg which, when opened, revealed a wooden carving of the Passion of Christ. This led to a renewal of interest in decorating eggs, many of which contained a surprise.

Over the next three centuries seemingly endless variations of decoration evolved and not only on the egg-shell itself. Wood was carved into the egg-shape and embellished with graceful traceries of colour, or had religious themes painted around as panels. Another material used was porcelain and glass too was used but the high point of all was the creation of the Russian Imperial eggs made by Fabergé. These are not only a symbol of eternity, they represent a time that is past.

2

First find your egg

Of all the birds' eggs that are available for decorating, the chicken egg is the most easily obtainable and has the advantage of being able to be used all the year round. It is, though, the most delicate, having a thin shell which is liable to shatter unexpectedly when cutting. Only by trial and error can one tell whether or not the chicken egg is too fragile to work with and this can be both time-wasting and expensive.

Cutting these small eggs *before* removing the contents supports the shell whilst it is under the pressure of being cut and this method can help. If the shell is not to be cut open and hinged later, but is to be decorated only on the outside, then it is better to hard boil the egg. About fifteen minutes should be enough and this will remove most of the grease from the outside of the shell. Hard-boiled eggs are not impervious to knocks and can still be cracked if dropped or tapped too hard, so care is needed when handling them.

Whether the chicken egg is brown or white does not matter when the surface is to be lacquered all over with a coloured lacquer. If the shell is to be painted, then the large white ones are the best as the white shell shows off the paint work, such as water colours, and gives a feeling of lightness. If the white shell is covered with clear lacquer afterwards, the painted white egg looks most convincingly like porcelain.

Duck eggs have a tougher shell than chicken eggs and they have a charming natural colour which ranges from off-white to the deepest duck-egg blue. There are also some black ones. Duck eggs can be handled with more firmness than can the chicken eggs but their size, being only slightly larger, confines decorative features to effects which are very simple, especially if using jewels and coloured roping. There is a limit too as to what can be put inside these small eggs as a surprise as the interiors are small and are difficult to make attractive by lining with silk or by building a small scene within.

A good egg size, though obtainable only with difficulty, are turkey eggs. These really are strong and can be quite large and are easily cut without breaking. The shells of turkey eggs 'manage' so well that one can go ahead with a fairly complex design with confidence.

Turkey eggs are speckled with brown dots and revealing this creates a pleasing effect, allowing the speckles to show through several layers of lacquer. To obliterate these speckles is difficult and several layers of coloured lacquer are needed before all trace of them has disappeared, though several layers of lacquer does give a wonderful lustre to the egg-shell.

The next size up the egg scale is the goose egg and on all counts this is the most suitable shell for cutting and for decorating. Its shell is thick and strong and its size, sometimes as large as 12.7cm tall, is ideal for cutting and for hiding surprises within.

The goose starts laying eggs on, or around, St Valentine's Day in February and it continues laying until June. The best eggs come along in April and May as by this time the goose's laying vent has become enlarged and, in consequence, the goose lays larger eggs.

Obtaining goose eggs is quite a problem. Even if one knows a friendly farmer, he will probably prefer to keep all his goose eggs as he would rather have the profit from the resultant geese than the price he would ask for the eggs. Farmers do have gluts though and so do people with small-holdings on which a few geese are reared. Sometimes the goose goes mad and lays eggs all over the place – she is called a silly goose. Silly indeed as these eggs are invariably infertile and would not hatch! Geese are unpredictable and often lay

6

frantically for no reason, thus a farmer might suddenly have more eggs than he wants or could afford to rear when hatched.

This is the time to make an offer to buy a few eggs. What is most difficult is knowing where the source of the eggs may be. Friends are the most useful fount of information and by keeping their eyes and ears open can tip one off about a likely place. Of one thing you can be certain – that when the goose eggs are located they will be miles from where you live. Sometimes it will be too costly either to fetch them or to have them sent.

Buying goose eggs unseen is not to be recommended. Out of a batch of goose eggs, only a few may be of the required large size. Many will be little larger than a turkey egg and therefore useless for creating the more elaborate designs upon.

There are eggs that are larger than those of the goose, such as the ostrich and emu and rhea. These are really large and beautiful but are not easily obtainable in Britain.

The ostrich egg is a cream colour and has a pitted surface, rather like an orange skin. The emu egg too has a pitted surface, but is shaped somewhat similar to a rugby ball, while the rhea egg is off-white and smooth and when sanded down has a lovely matt finish.

I was given one of these large egg-shells once, though the event was not without incident.

The wife of a friend of mine, who had been visiting Australia, wrote to me asking if there was something she could bring back for me. I could think of nothing I wanted from Australia, except perhaps a ticket to go there and see the country for myself. Then I had an idea and wrote back to her and asked her to try and bring me an emu's egg.

I didn't know then what a fuss I would be starting. She told me that she had to travel to the 'outbush' where there was an emu farm and buy a freshly laid emu egg. Then she had to take it back to Sydney and with the help of a friend, a bicycle pump, a hammer and an electric drill, she had the task of evacuating the contents of the egg. This nearly made them both sick. They then boiled the shell and removed all the mucus from inside and when it was dry packed it lightly in a cardboard box ready for carrying aboard the plane.

There had just been a spate of hijackings and personal baggage was being vigorously inspected. My friend's wife was on a stopping plane and, wishing to stretch her legs at every opportunity and not daring to leave the egg on the seat unattended, she took the box with her and had to show it to a succession of suspicious security men, all of whom thought the dark green ovoid was a bomb!

I think these large eggs are better left in their natural state. Their very size and unusualness is enough to make them a decorative feature. It is possible to cut and hinge them, but they are unwieldy, and if covered in jewels look gross and rather vulgar.

Wild bird eggs are protected by law and should not be used. In fact most are too small to be effectively decorated. There are some eggs which can be used, though infinite patience and most delicate handling is needed for any success. Such eggs as quail or pigeon, providing they are large specimens, can look interesting if treated simply. They are, however, tricky to handle and if given away as a present will soon be returned for 'repairs', a job often impossible and always tedious.

After trying many different sorts of egg-shells I have found that the most adaptable is the goose egg. It has strength, a reliable shape and can be the perfect size. Finding a supply of goose eggs is the problem though, but is another challenge in the art of decorating eggs.

3

Equipment

Scissors   Ones you are used to using are best. Button scissors can be helpful, so too can those with curved blades.

Tweezers   For placing decoration on shells and items within the shell.

Pincers   For cutting or severing through old jewellery.

Pliers   For shaping wire or rods or for holding objects whilst filing, etc.

Small vice   For holding difficult-to-cut-by-hand pieces. This can come in useful in many ways and need not be mounted on a bench. Try and buy a second-hand one.

Fret-saw with metal cutting blade   For sawing through brass fittings, jewellery, wood and many items.

Files   Small sharp files for altering old jewellery, filing down unwanted particles such as brooch clasps.

Serrated knife   For cutting the shell. One fine and one coarse.

Razor blade   Single-edged ones are best. Useful for severing the egg membrane, cutting cord, edge, etc.

Tooth brush   For cleaning out inside of the shell and for brushing baize lining to the underside of the base.

Pencil   For marking cutting lines.

Eraser   For cleaning shell and for removing pencil marks.

Glue   Araldite Rapid. Uhu. Pritt Cream. Always replace cap of tubes otherwise much will be wasted.

Blu-Tack   Useful for picking up small jewels. Make into a fine point by wrapping around the point of a toothpick or match stick, then use as a 'magnet' to pick up a jewel or pearl and place into position.

Nail polish   As many bottles of as many different colours as can be obtained. Three bottles of the *same* colour may be needed to cover a large goose egg-shell.

Clear nail polish   Used as a final glaze, preserving both the decoration and the gilding.

Nail polish remover   Useful for cleaning paint brushes and for removing excess glue and coloured nail polish.

Paper towels   Using these when holding a shell will prevent the grease from the hand covering the shell. Other uses are obvious.

Paint brushes   Small sizes, about six in all. Keep two for applying liquid gold leaf and two for silver. The others use for colour, cleaning after use.

Sandpaper   For cleaning and smoothing the surface of the shell, also for finishing off filed jewellery.

Magnifying glass   For checking accuracy of design. Also for inspecting pieces of jewellery and prints that will be used for découpage.

Needles   For piercing the egg-shell of goose eggs that seem weak, or those of the hen. Also for sewing the linings.

Egg boxes   Many uses: standing shells in when drying lacquer, for storing smaller shells, for storing different coloured jewels, etc.

Large piece of rag   Always at hand for cleaning fingers.

Small piece of rag   To wipe off excess Araldite and other glues. Discard when dirty.

Bradawl   For piercing hole in the ends of eggs prior to blowing.

Hammer   For tapping the bradawl and useful for altering shape of metal items, beating lightly on the iron of the vice.

4

Goose Eggs: Blowing and storing

Goose eggs are difficult to obtain and are, therefore, to be treasured even before decorating.

After obtaining a supply the eggs have to be prepared for decorating, either immediately or at a later date.

If the finished design is known and the egg's shape is suitable then the shell can be cut at once, whilst the egg is still inside. After the cutting process, which may be either a door or all around the shell, the contents can be easily emptied out and the shell cleaned inside and outside with cold water and a toothbrush.

The disadvantage of this is that it *almost* prevents hingeing the shell before finally cutting it (see 14, Hingeing), and this pre-cutting method of hingeing is desirous because it ensures that each half of the shell will close together exactly. I say *almost* because if one is very careful the shell can be kept dry of albumen seeping through the hinge-cut and a hinge can be fixed into place. More often than not, though, the shell will have sweated beneath the glue used to attach the hinge and will eventually cause the hinge to become loose.

A better way of preparing the shell is to blow out the contents which is a cheek-aching task but one that is rewarding in the end as those eggs not immediately needed for decoration are ready to store and cut later.

To blow out the contents make a hole at either end of the shell. This prevents a vacuum from building up inside. A goose egg is quite strong and will stand quite a tap. Take a hammer and a bradawl and tap until through the shell and the inner membrane. A quite large hole may be made through the narrow end of the shell as this end will eventually be seated in position on a base and will then be unseen. This large (approx ½cm) hole makes the blowing process much easier. It also breaks up the contents, making them, if fresh, only fit for scrambling or making omelettes.

Having mentioned cooking, it must be said that though the goose egg tastes little different from a hen's egg, cooking it gives a result harder and more coagulated when scrambled and, if used in a sponge, can make a very heavy cake. If the shell is cut and not blown and the contents emptied out carefully without breaking the yolk, it nearly fills a frying pan and makes a delicious breakfast. One goose egg is equivalent to three hen's eggs.

After blowing out the contents leave the shell to dry out thoroughly. A good resting place is on an egg box. When the shell is dry (or shells, if you are lucky and you are preparing a quantity), a good place to store the shells is in a cardboard box, marking the outside with 'small' and 'large'. Shoe boxes are a convenient size and fit onto most shelves. I grade my shells and save the really large ones for special designs, using the smaller ones first, both to practise on and to work off some of the ideas that are in my mind. The smaller shells can be really beautiful providing they are mounted on a base which is in proportion to their size and the jewellery applied is not too heavy or opulent.

5
Design

To cut and decorate a design on so perfect an object as an egg may be said to be tampering with nature; but why not? It is good fortune indeed to have so perfect a shape as a starting point on which to base a design.

First, look at the egg and observe its proportions. Each egg, though basically an egg-shape, is different and though these differences are slight, they will affect the final design. Look at the examples in Figure 1.

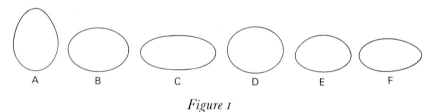

Figure 1

A, D, and F would be suitable for an upright design, such as shown in Figure 2,

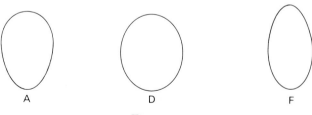

Figure 2

and B, C, and E are more adaptable to horizontal mounting, as in Figure 3.

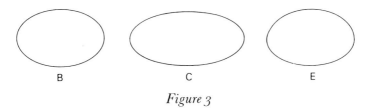

B　　　　　　　C　　　　　　　E

Figure 3

The shape of the egg-shell also dictates where the cut will go. If it is to be a casket, for instance, then on shell A, in order to achieve a balanced effect, the cut should be below the centre line, giving the upper half of the shell a good area of 'dome' to adorn (Figure 4).

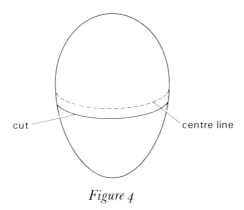

cut　　　　　　　　　　　centre line

Figure 4

Egg-shape D would be more suitable for a door opening as the shell is squat and has plenty of width.

Egg-shape F, being more elongated and taller, needs a cut just above the centre. This gives depth in the lower half and is fine for hiding surprises, or is deep enough to take a miniature figure on a stand.

The scale of the upper half to the lower half is important as the design must look harmonious when the shell is opened or closed (Figure 5).

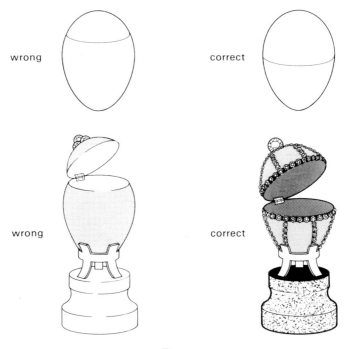

Figure 5

After deciding upon an appropriate cut – it may be a lid opening or a door – the design of the shell, stand and base must all be in harmony. It is bad design, for instance, to incorporate differing styles or to use colours that clash. Think about what effect you wish to achieve and then make notes as an aid to your memory. You may think a particular egg-shell will be suitable as a jewelled casket and you decide that its shape suggests cutting it horizontally.

After deciding on a basic colour, look through your materials and find matching or blending items that will help in creating your ideas and all be in harmony. As an egg-shell is quite fragile, paint the basic colour onto a piece of stiff white paper – an area of about 2 cm square will be enough. This piece of paper can now be your matching sample. You can take it from room to room, looking through drawers or in cupboards for a piece of material or some trinket.

16

Against this test colour sample you must try linings and jewels, beads, etc. and gold cording for trimming. The gold is important because it comes in many different shades and using the right one is important. There is Antique Gold, Old Gold, Bright Gold, Gold Leaf light, Gold Leaf dark, in fact there are a surprising number of shades of gold, just as in real gold. Nine-carat gold has more copper in it than, say, 22-carat, hence it is dark and orangy, whereas 22-carat gold is bright and yellowy.

With the test paper to guide you, gather together all the things that harmonise with it. The colour may be pink; then look out 'pearls', pale green stones from a brooch, imitation diamonds, light 'sapphires', opals and moonstones, etc. These would harmonise with the pink. Onyx or garnets or imitation rubies, or dark blue glass brilliants would be inappropriate. For some effects, the shine of black jet could be a foil against pink.

You are now ready to decide on how these things will fit into your original thinking about design. Refer back to your notes and read again your thoughts.

Is your egg going to be in the style of rococo, or the eighteenth century, or be Victorian in feeling, or modern, or none of these but just something of your own fancy? Whatever the intention, the effect will be easier if you first of all assemble all the things you need.

Remember, too, the relative size of an egg. It is a small area to decorate in whatever style you choose and it is all too easy to get carried away and over-decorate, thereby destroying the original intention and ending up with something that pleases no one, least of all yourself; it is you who will have done all the work.

Restraint is the solution for it is better to under-decorate than to over-decorate. An example of over-decoration is using thick, wide lampshade braid to encircle the shell. This material is inappropriate as it always looks what it is, and itself was designed for lampshades, not for the delicate trimming of an egg-shell. It should be avoided at all costs. I have seen heavily trimmed, dark-coloured egg-shells that have looked more like hand grenades than the light attractive objects they should be.

When thinking about a design for the lid of an upright jewel casket, remember restraint and try and avoid the effects shown in Figure 6 A and B.

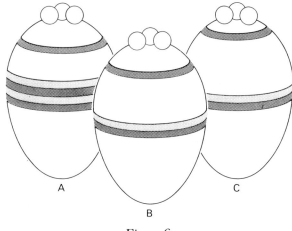

Figure 6

The design A is top heavy, there are too many rows of trimming of whatever kind above the cut line and this destroys the proportion of the upper half of the egg-shell. Design B has too much distance between the trim above the cut line and that beneath the finial, which itself is set too close to the finial. Design C seems to be satisfying in proportion.

The design C is one of many alternatives on the same idea, that of encircling the egg-shell with trimming of varying widths and of varying textures. Whatever trim is used, though, the height and width of the egg-shell should govern the amount used.

Do not forget when designing an egg-shell that it is three-dimensional and not a flat surface similar to the paper you may have drawn some ideas on. Therefore, remember the rear of the egg-shell, where the hinge will be fixed, and allow for either altering the actual appearance of the hinge, or covering it over. The 'back' of the decorated egg-shell should be as beautiful and as carefully planned and executed as the front. This is particularly relevant when think-

18

ing about encircling the cut line with braid or roping or any kind of trim and consideration must be given to the hinge.

The hinge will stand proud of the egg-shell by about 1.6mm and this small distance can be filled in by glueing layers of paper at either side, onto the shell and building it up to the level of the hinge. Alternatively, wide gold banding can be used, if it is of the same colour as the rest of your gold trimming. Araldite, too, can be laid on thickly at either side of the hinge, building up the distance with a thick layer which is very strong.

When practised in decorating egg-shells and remembering proportion and perspective and period, greater freedom of design can be indulged; you can go a bit wild. Observing the rule of restraint and being aware of the actual size and shape of the egg-shell you are working on, whatever fancy strikes you will have some sort of harmony. Your eye and hand will have become accustomed to working with your materials and you will have a definite feel for good design.

Design does not stop at the actual egg-shell. The stand and the base must be considered when first thinking of the total effect and thought must be given to colour and shape or form, size and appropriateness of base and stand. One should avoid effects such as those shown in Figure 7, the faults of which will be obvious – either the base is too big for the egg-shell or vice versa.

Compare the egg-shell first with the base to be used, also the stand. A good yardstick is to divide the whole assembled decorated

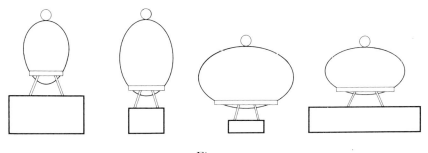

Figure 7

egg-shell, stand and base into three approximately equal parts, one third being the distance from the top of the finial to the cut line, or, if a door cut, then to the centre of the door. A second third measures from the cut line to the top of the base and the base makes up the last third, as shown in Figure 8.

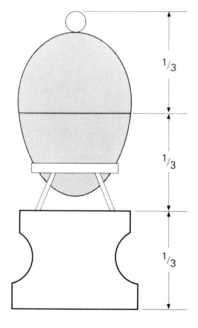

$^1/_3$

$^1/_3$

$^1/_3$

Figure 8

6
Guidelines in attaining good design

Proportion The egg-shell, stand and base should be in proportion to each other and not one obviously larger than the other.

Style Decide on what effect you want to achieve and stick to it, e.g. Opulent, Fussy, Feminine, Simple.

Period If trying an eighteenth-century effect, then become familiar with the period idiosyncrasies and copy them. For baroque use bows and Greek key patterns, garlands of flowers, maybe, or golden borders, harps and trophies. For Victorian, heavier effects are needed – crosses, single flowers, cut-outs and scraps découpaged on to the egg-shell. Use more opulent jewellery; deeper colours may be preferred. Try Egyptian or Chinese or Indian, read up about their design features, or those of any other period. Look out for 'findings' that are appropriate and use trimmings that are sympathetic.

Gold Use only one colour of gold on an egg-shell unless a deliberate contrast is intended.

Trimmings Be consistent in colour, harmonise the lining and the colour of the egg-shell. They need not be the same but too much contrast can be a disaster. A pale-green egg-shell lined with pale heliotrope or oyster silk is fine, but if the egg-shell is lined with navy-blue silk, no matter how expensive or antique it is, the result would not be harmonious.

Size Remember the smallness of the finished creation. Each design feature must work for its place and be seen. Be clean and clear in your intention.

Care Take care when doing each process – glueing or cutting and fixing the lining, setting the hinge or applying the lacquer. Care of execution shows in the end and lack of this can spoil a good idea.

7

Cutting: Straight cuts

Cutting a goose egg-shell need not present a problem if one is careful and has unshaking, firm hands. No machines are necessary, though a small power drill can be used. I use a serrated stainless steel knife or a fine metal saw blade. I prefer the knife, though, as, being designed for kitchen use it has an easy-to-hold handle. There are many small knives available and I would advise purchasing one that is most suitable to your own grip. I use one especially designed by the manufacturer for cutting tomatoes, but there are many others. It is largely a case of experiment and before purchasing any knife I would suggest looking in a kitchen drawer. Very often some unused knife will be found pushed to the back and will come into use in a different way from that for which it was bought. These serrated knives can be re-sharpened using a household steel, as one would re-sharpen a carving knife, and for shell cutting they should be constantly re-sharpened as the shell textures wear the blade down quickly.

A razor blade is also useful for finally severing any awkward pieces of egg membrane and also for gently easing open the cut shell that has previously been hinged. I use the single-sided ones as they are safer. A packet of five will last as many years.

To make a straight line around the waist of a shell, a simple method is to put a thick rubber band around it, in the position you wish the cut to be, then pencil around the band-line. A thickish band will not slip as would a thin one.

After cutting, make a pencil dash across each half shell then each half can be placed together again accurately.

For fitting a hinge *before* cutting, see 14, 'Hingeing',

The wider end of the shell should be uppermost.

Figure 9 shows an orthodox cut, roughly dividing the shell into two equal parts. The upper half should be slightly smaller than the lower because (see dots) this will be set within some sort of base. There will then be a better proportion to the finished design.

Figure 10 shows a lower cut which affords a larger area for decorating and a really deep inner lid that can take a pleated or ruched lining and will still enable the lid to close upon an upstanding 'surprise'. The base line is shown by the dots.

Figure 11 shows a high cut which more or less resembles a trap-lid and is only really useful as an opening to a dropped compartment for jewellery, or to frame a photo or print. The fixing of a finial to such a shell is made difficult and much thought should precede starting on such a design.

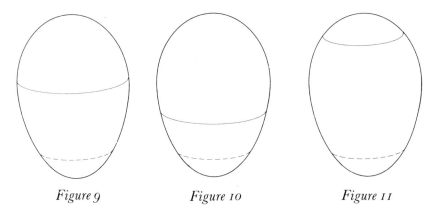

Figure 9   *Figure 10*   *Figure 11*

Before thinking about decoration or colour, thought should be given as to a suitable cut for the *shape* and *size* of an egg-shell. Goose eggs come in all sizes and only the larger ones can support the more complicated cuts; also each egg-*shape* differs; see Figure 12.

Figure 13 would be unsuitable for cutting to mount on its side as a casket as it is too pointed.

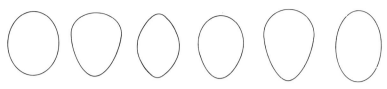

Figure 12

Figure 14 shows a very satisfying shape for a centre, straight waist-cut, having a spreading dome, 'A', and a generous lower half to

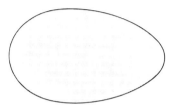

Figure 13

enable either a compartment to be made for jewellery, or a place in which to put a surprise.

Figure 14

8
Cutting: Curved cuts

All cuts other than the plain circular waist-cut need to be carefully thought out beforehand, to avoid design difficulties. It is useless to cut a complicated curve as part of a design and then have no clear idea as to what effect you are aiming at. Simplicity is the key-note of good design, but so often it is fun to experiment and to do something out of the ordinary. It is no bad thing to experiment, but as I say, think out the complete shell design *before* starting the *design*, not the decoration. The proportion of shell to stand and of stand and shell to base is all-important. (See 15, Bases.)

The curved cuts I have shown are only a few of the many possibilities and they are the simplest. Those which form a point need very careful handling and decorating. The point is most vulnerable and once chipped off is extremely difficult to replace.

The curved-cut shells do make attractive jewel caskets and look very pretty but be warned, the more complicated the cut the more hazardous and difficult is the lining of the upper shell. Do not waste time and start something you cannot finish, instead, make any amount of plain-cut or straight-cut designs first and make a mental note of where *you*, yourself, experience difficulty. If it is when fixing the inside lining (see 19, Linings), which can be tricky, then be cautious about being too adventurous when tracing a curved line for cutting.

Do not forget that when decorating shells, whatever process you are attempting, strive for the best and most careful possible result. Finished designs attract much attention and lack of scrutiny and

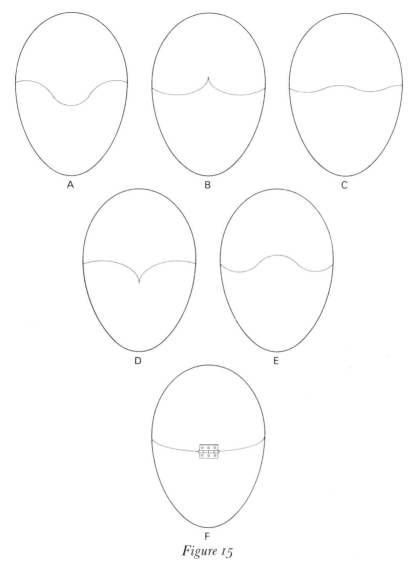

Figure 15

careless workmanship will show up. I say this because an egg design can take a great deal of time and thought to complete and the result should be worth the effort. If you take care, *you* will be pleased.

The rear view of all those curved cuts shown, is as illustrated by example F, and is straight where the hinge fits.

9
Cutting: For side mounting

The shell, when cut around its length for mounting on its side, can either be cut at the centre (1), or around the top (2), or around the lower half (3), depending on how the finished design is envisaged. Of the three alternatives, Figure 16.3 is a more attractive cut as it shows a larger upper half, good for decoration and allows a full silk lining to be fitted easily. Also it will support a fair-sized finial without it looking too heavy (4).

A holding chain to prevent the lid opening too wide should be fitted. See 14, Hingeing.

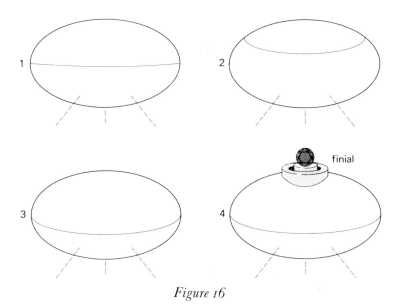

Figure 16

10
Cutting: The door cut

Doors cut into egg-shells are best kept as simple as possible. The plain circle (Figure 17. 1) is ideal for the beginner but care should be taken to place the circle in the centre of the actual shell outline.

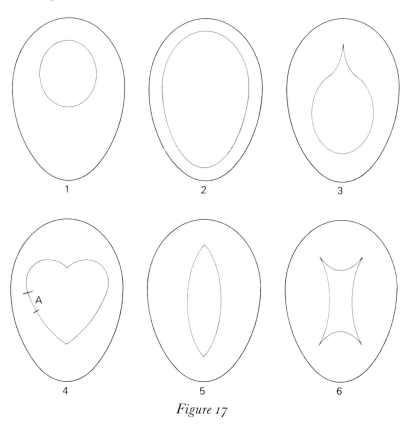

Figure 17

In Figure 17.2 the shell is almost cut in half, giving a very wide-opening door. This is suitable for showing scenes or groups of figures within.

The pointed outline (Figure 17.3) has an oriental feel and is a suitable frame for, say, a Chinese figure or an arrangement of blue and white flowers.

The heart-shaped door (Figure 17.4) is tricky, one has to 'manage' or elongate slightly the hinge side (A) to take the hinge. This eccentricity can be disguised by the final trimming.

The elongated oval of Figure 17.5 is useful as a surprise door, concealed in the final layers of trimming and jewels. Care should be taken to conceal the hinge, or there will not *be* a surprise door!

Design 17.6 is quite impractical although it looks interesting. There is no secure place to which to attach a hinge. It is a pretty design, but only on paper. To cut an egg-shell and then find it impractical to hinge is not only a waste of time but a waste of a good shell, often so hard to come by. I speak from experience as I have cut several such fanciful designs and have had to learn by my mistakes.

11
Cutting: Complicated cuts

Whatever the craft, people will always enjoy a challenge, even seek one, and egg decorators are no exception. Personally, I do not care very much for the more complicated ways of cutting shells. Proportion and balance are difficult to achieve and the result is often very fragile and has a short life.

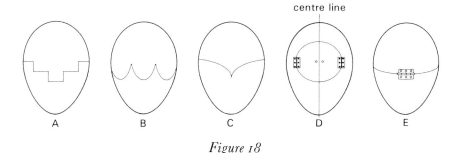

Figure 18

Here, though (Figure 18), are some possible yet eccentric cuts. The first three are all hinged at the back as shown in figure E. They need caution and careful cutting, making sure to work slowly and finish the final cutting with a razor blade going well up into the points and angles. A coat of clear acetate lacquer will strengthen these cut shells either for immediate working on, or for storage for later use. Two coats are better and will really make those tricky corners and points much stronger and less liable to fracture or to break off.

Shell D has a double door at the front, with each hinge position marked. The door must be drawn *exactly* in a central position on the shell and the hinges fixed before final cutting, otherwise either they will be crooked or will not close together correctly.

Measure around the centre circumference of the shell and divide by two. This will give a centre point. Mark this point, then measure from it to left and to right, the width you wish the doors to be, then draw a circle using the outer measurement as a guide. This will position the doors centrally.

12

Cutting: An 'impossible' cut

An 'impossible' cut and one which has driven many an egg decorator distracted yet continues to fascinate and to challenge, is the petal or lotus cut.

Take a large, slender-shaped goose egg-shell and place around it two wide rubber bands, as shown in Figure 19 A.

For this design the shell should be cut with the pointed end uppermost.

Having made sure the bands are equally separated around the shell so that each division is equal, mark each on the same side (see dots) with a pencil line. Remove the bands and you will have a shell divided into four parts. Now divide the egg around its lower waist, using a rubber band (see Figure 19 B). You will now have eight sections of shell. Cut each vertical line downwards towards the horizontal one (Figure 19 C – first cut line). Now make a small cut where the four hinges will be placed and set the hinges into position with Araldite, allowing twenty-four hours for setting. Then cut around the rest of the horizontal line (see Figure 19 C – second cut line), and the four segments will separate and fold outwards like petals, or a lotus.

You will now have achieved the difficult petal cut, hinged and ready for decoration in a suitable style.

Cover the whole outside of the shell parts with two layers of strengthening clear acetate lacquer; hard high-gloss nail polish is a good medium. Leave these layers to set perfectly hard.

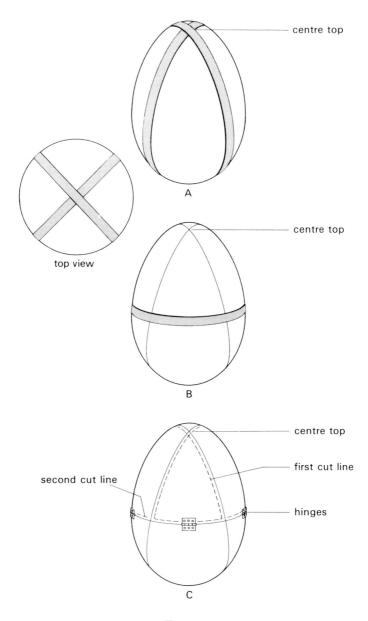

centre top

top view

A

centre top

B

centre top

first cut line

second cut line

hinges

C

Figure 19

Whatever design you decide upon keep it very simple. It may be a ballet theme or a Chinese theme or Indian, or may have inside a bouquet of flowers as a surprise when the petals are opened. The inside must not be overshadowed by the outer decoration. As I say, keep it simple, without overdoing the trimmings.

I have made this cut but have never been pleased with the result, either feeling the end product was too fragile to touch or that each segment, in spite of great care, was not of the same size *exactly*, thus destroying the harmony of the whole.

The egg, whilst being perfect as an ovoid shape, can have unequal corners which, if divided into two, will differ like the human face, each half will be quite different in shape; it may only be a fraction but enough to spoil what may have been thirty hours of work.

Cut away, though, and invent whatever fantasies you can, but be advised that to be simple is best. Your design and finish can then support as much complex decoration as you can devise.

13

Drawers

Inserting small drawers into egg-shell designs is a very tricky business and when a design is being worked out needs a lot of thought.

For instance, is the drawer to be in the upper half or the lower half of the shell? Is the shell to have both opening (a door) and a drawer? Will there be two drawers? How large will the drawer be in proportion to the egg and relative to the overall design? Most of all though, will the drawer open and close easily and will it hold something? A drawer is, after all, designed to hold something and if you design one into which it is impossible to put anything, or one that is too fragile to be opened often and freely, then the effect and effort will have been wasted.

As a drawer is most fiddly to construct and to place into position it is necessary to plan very carefully before starting.

First, check whether or not the depth of the shell is wide enough to allow the size of drawer that you want. Having done this, mark on the shell the outline of the drawer, below or above the cut line, as you wish (see Figure 20).

Now decide what will be most suitable for use as the actual drawer. Old match boxes are good, especially the small ones such as can be bought in Italy and which hold small wax matches. A drawer, though, is not very difficult to make yourself, from thin cardboard and this way you can be sure you have one the exact size you wish.

To do this, first of all cut the sides of the drawer and stick them together with small pieces of Sellotape (see shaded area, Figure 21).

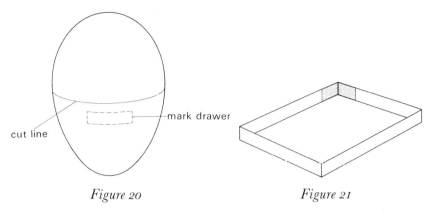

cut line

mark drawer

Figure 20   *Figure 21*

Now measure the bottom and fix in position in the same way, with Sellotape. *Always* put the Sellotape on the *inside* of the box or drawer, thereby causing no obstruction on the *outside*.

The drawer is now ready and, as you are now sure of its size, you can place it against the mark you have made on the shell and draw around its exact size, making the outline in the position where you wish it to open.

When cutting the shell, cut a fraction larger than your outline. Do this by cutting to the *outside* edge of your pencil line. This will allow your drawer to move more freely.

As soon as you have cut out the shell opening, coat the cut shell piece with two or three layers of clear lacquer. Clear nail varnish is ideal. This will strengthen the piece and will help prevent any mishap. The tiny piece will be convex, the same as the shape of the egg-shell and will eventually be glued to the outside front of the drawer, so guard it carefully as no substitute will fit.

A drawer must have a support, or a platform underneath it so that it can slide easily in and out and it must have a platform above, so as to prevent the drawer rising when being pushed in. These two platforms form a guide into which the drawer is pushed and are made by cutting cardboard to the correct measurement of the interior above and below the drawer opening. They are glued into place. As the top platform conceals the drawer from above, the egg-shell can be double cut, as, for example, in Figure 22.

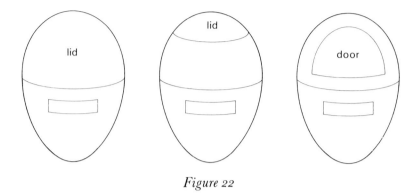

Figure 22

Figure 23 shows the drawer in its position inside the shell and between the two platforms.

To make sure the drawer runs smoothly, rub a little talcum powder onto the top of the lower platform.

To prevent the drawer from pulling right out each time it is opened, cut a small strip of silk (or cotton, but silk is more pliable) to the length of the drawer and glue one end of the strip onto the back of the drawer and the other end onto the rear on the inside of the egg-shell *before* inserting the platform above the drawer. When the glued silk strip has set, it will prevent the drawer pulling out more than just less than its own length.

The piece of cut shell has to be glued onto the front of the drawer and after this has been done there will be a gap between the shell and the drawer. Fill this in with either plaster or Araldite, anything you have to hand, and then cover with a piece of paper or silk.

Line the drawer with a suitable material, fiddly again, but essential for a good effect. Now the drawer is ready for decorating on the outside.

Thin gold cording is ideal for edging the drawer and for a knob maybe a single claw-set 'diamond', or a tiny gold dress shirt stud will serve. You will see something that is suitable amongst your findings. Be sure that it is in harmony with your overall design and in proportion to both the egg-shell size and the base, stand and finial.

38

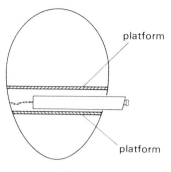

Figure 23

Assembly plan for including a drawer:

1. Make the drawer.
2. Cut outline in shell.
3. Mount bottom platform inside shell.
4. Rub talcum powder into upper surface of lower platform.
5. Line the inside of the drawer.
6. Glue piece of egg-shell on to front of drawer.
7. Fill in gap between shell and drawer.
8. Fix silk strip to prevent drawer pulling out.
9. Glue into position the platform above the drawer.

The drawer is now fixed into position and will slide in and out smoothly.

14

Hingeing

Apart from cutting, hingeing is the next important procedure when preparing the egg-shell. The hinge must be set correctly in position without any excess glue fouling the hinge pin (see Figure 24 B).

After marking the shell with a pencil where it will finally be cut (see Figure 24 A), mark the position where the hinge will be placed and then cut either side of the area (see dotted line). Cut well to either side of the hinge measurements as this will be difficult of access once the hinge is set in position.

The position on the shell where the hinge will be seated should first be sand-papered clean, as should the underside of the hinge itself; this removes any 'factory finish' and reveals the plain metal, brass or copper.

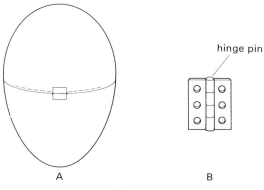

A   B

Figure 24

Using a quick-set glue such as Araldite Rapid, apply a little to both the surface of the shell and the hinge and allow each to stand until slightly hard, then place the hinge in position and firm down. Make sure that the hinge pin is level with the cut line; if you do not, the egg will open in a crooked manner.

Often a hinge will need adjustment when setting, so do not use one of the 'instant-set' adhesives. Araldite Rapid is most suitable, though I could wish it would not 'string-out' like chewing gum. Be careful of this stringing, it can be avoided if one works slowly.

Figure 25 shows suggested positions for hinges. A, B and C are straightforward. D will need careful handling when opening. E, care should be taken to see that it will open *after* trimming and

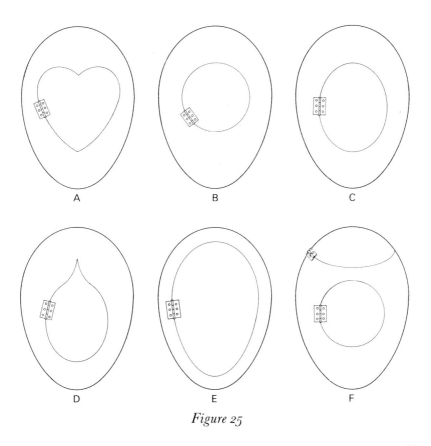

Figure 25

will also open clear of the base to which it is fixed. F shows a double door arrangement, an opening at the top and a door at the front.

When making any egg which opens as a lid, it is advisable to fix a holding chain inside to prevent the lid falling open too wide. Attach a fine piece of chain to the inside bottom and top with Araldite Rapid, judging the exact position by slowly working the lid up and down (Figure 26).

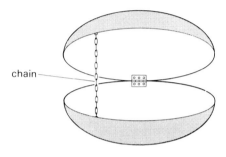

Figure 26

Plates

1 'David' This egg is covered with emerald-green lacquer and trimmed with Tiffany-set amethysts

2 'David' egg opened, showing miniature head of Michaelangelo's David lacquered in purple. The lid is lined with silk and studded with diamonds and glass tears

3 'Moghul' An oyster-lacquered shell patterned with pearls, topaz and citrines. The caparison on the lid is of turquoise. The stand is a double lotus set with diamonds and the base is of oak decorated with Moghul motifs

4 'Moghul' egg opened, showing a miniature Taj Mahal in ivory. The egg weights ¾lb or 300 grammes

5 'Harmony' A shell exposed, showing its natural fine off-white colour. The trimming is quite simple, being of gold altar roping and diamonds from an Edwardian ball gown. The baby as a finial is made of bisque and is from a Victorian wedding cake. It has been covered in gold leaf

6 'Harmony', when open, reveals a small etched silver vase containing a miniature bouquet of dried flowers. The egg is lined with heliotrope silk of 1920 and has the birth sign of Aries hidden under the vase stand. It is a musical egg and plays Boccherini's 'Minuet'

7 'Children Playing' This shell is coated in pearl lacquer and has Victorian scraps set *en découpage* under the final glazing. Inside, the children are arranged amidst natural grasses. The whole is set on an early Waterford wine-glass stem

8 'Nativity' The lacquer is the blue of the Holy Mother's gown. The trimmings are simple gold braid and ball-roping. Bishop's cope ribbon is set on the base. The egg is musical and plays 'Adeste Fidelis'

9 'Bird's Nest' A heart-shaped door of oyster lacquer opens to reveal two infertile blackbird eggs on a nest of heather, clematis and moss. The bird is gilded Victorian bisque. The base is set with peacock-blue bugles taken from a 1930s dress

10 'Hommage à l'Homme' Naked Greek figures entwine around the ivory-white lacquer. The finial is a large glass orb. The 'emeralds' are Tiffany-set, supported with gold braid. Under the glass base is set a Greek warrior seated on the back of a lion. Inside is a montage of the naked male form

11 'Angels' Angels guard the Manger. The inside has birds and beasts set against a colourful background. The doors are trimmed with sapphires. The base is turned from apple-wood and trimmed with silk altar ribbon

12 'Geranium' The shell was painted with acrylic paint before the flowers were painted. The whole is covered in ten layers of clear lacquer.

The stand is oak and the finial is a diamond-studded Victorian hat-pin. The inside is lined with oyster silk and filled with flowers and perfumed with oil of geranium

13 'Swan'   The egg is gilded and lacquered and has oyster shells cascading down onto the swan's back. The swan is set on a carved stand and has jewellery set around i.e., pearls, moonstone and topaz. The top of the stand is a mirror. The finial is made of two intaglio earrings

14 'Swan' egg opened. Inside lined with pink taffeta and has a 'snowstorm' as the surprise. Inside the tiny glass sphere is an arrangement of mountain flowers in porcelain. The egg is musical and plays 'Edelweiss'

15 'Green Casket'   Apple-green lacquer coats an egg in which are set four Victorian winged childs' faces. The finial is an opal. Inside the lid, set in a ring of diamonds and gold roping, is a coloured oval panel showing lovers meeting. The casket is lined with blue velvet

16 'Elizabeth'   An egg made to commemorate the eightieth birthday of Queen Elizabeth, the Queen Mother. The base is carved ebony and the stand has garlands of roses to support the oyster-lacquered egg. The finial is an ivory lion, the hinges covered with intaglio bows

17 (*left*) 'Cupid'   This biscuit-coloured egg is lined with apricot silk and stands on a beechwood base. The surprise inside is a bouquet of Royal Doulton flowers set on a seed-head of Love-in-the-Mist
(*right*) 'Lovers'   An eighteenth-century stipple engraving is découpaged on to the door of the egg. Inside, Cupid stands on a plinth, surrounded by Love-in-the-Mist flower petals

18 'Cornelian'   A jewel casket in cornelian lacquer. The finial is a gold dolphin. The egg is trimmed with gold cording and turquoise bugles. Inside the lid and set in pearls is a painting by Boucher of a naked lady reclining on a bed. Under the egg, the curved base has a scene of lovers pleading

19 (*left*) 'Wheatspray'   This egg has a Moghul-inspired cut, with an intaglio wheatspray on the door
(*right*) 'Topaz Moghul'   This similarly inspired egg has a smoky topaz from Jaipur, India, set on green lacquer. Inside, a gold bird is alighting on a field of cotton-tail grass. The stand sits on an ebony circle

20 'Topaz Moghul'   The topaz door opens to reveal an interior of shells and flowers and pale mauve feathers. Set on the door are two children under a gilded glaze

21 'Royal Wedding'   An egg made in frosted pink lacquer and gold to mark the wedding of the Prince and Princess of Wales. The bisque baby

inside is set in a garland of flowers and sits on a stand; the whole lifts out. The jewels are rhinestones and pearls

22 'Florence' A black, diamond and shot-blue/red lacquered egg on a black lacquer base. Inside is a model of Florence Cathedral

23 'Amethyst' An egg of amethyst lacquer and silver trimming. Inside, mother-of-pearl birds are in a nest of silver lace and heliotrope silk. The base is ebony, the egg set on a silver gallery

24 (*left*) 'Children Playing', showing door closed (see 7)
(*right*) 'Millinery' This yellow egg has on it découpage work of period hats. Inside is an arrangement of Victorian flowers and jet buttons, the whole set on an ebony base.

1, 2

3, 4

5, 6

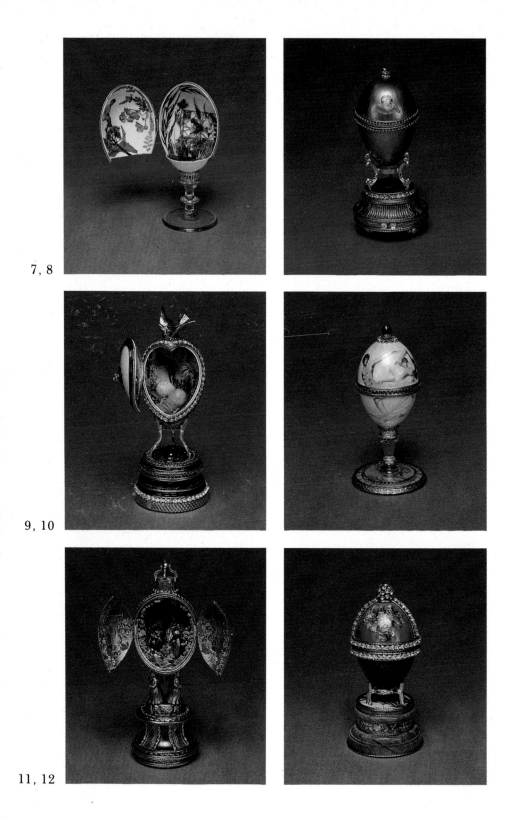

7, 8

9, 10

11, 12

13, 14

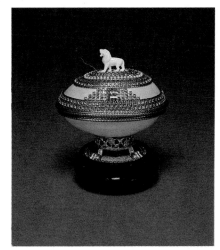

15, 16

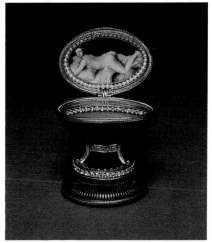

17, 18

19, 20

21, 22

23, 24

15

Bases and stands

The base is that part of the overall design that supports the stand which, in turn, supports the actual shell, and there are as many different shapes for bases as the mind can imagine. The fifteen designs shown in Figure 30 took me less than two minutes to sketch out; obviously the variety is infinite.

The most readily available material from which to make a base is wood – oak or mahogany or deal, any old wood in fact – because the finished base shape is covered with decoration unless the grain of the wood is so attractive that it is worth making a feature. Unless one is going to carve out a wooden base, one needs access to a lathe. The shape can be made of cardboard though, cutting, bending and glueing more simple shapes together in order to form some of the more basic patterns, such as the drum-shape. Base number 11 (Figure 30) is a very similar shape to the large cotton bobbin and many crafters will have such a bobbin in a needlework box which, if it is sanded down and lacquered black, makes an ideal base for supporting one of the smaller goose shells, or a turkey shell.

The actual support, or stand, into which the shell is fixed with Araldite can be obtained in a variety of designs from craft shops and department stores, though they take some searching out and can be expensive.

Patterns such as those shown in Figure 27 can be obtained and are usually sold for supporting the marble or jade eggs one can buy.

Other supports can be made from literally anything – bottle tops, nail-varnish tops, indeed any top from anything.

Figure 27

Figure 28 shows but some of the enormous range available in every conceivable size, and below is an example of how they might be used, together with a base, as illustrated in Figure 30, and an egg-shell (Figure 29).

a medicine bottle cap

typical nail-polish stopper

the top off a perfume bottle

Figure 28

One should aim to make the base and stand harmonise in form and support the shell as though they belonged together. To use the first example of an improvised stand, the nail-polish stopper, on the base design number 5 (Figure 30) would be incongruous.

Experimentation is to be encouraged. Use and experiment with whatever is to hand and you will achieve some very pleasing effects, but always remember your proportions, shell to stand to base.

Again I stress the need for the sort of careful workmanship that will be satisfying and lasting. At this stage, when the shell and stand and base have been decided upon, each item should be finished individually as perfectly as possible. The shell must be sanded to a fine finish, the hinge prepared correctly and fixed to the shell exactly

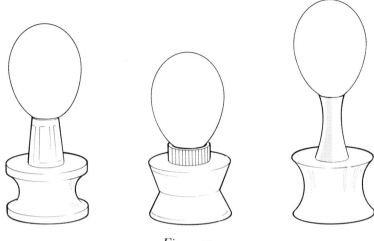

Figure 29

in position, the stand and the base be in harmony and sandpapered or polished, and both be *in proportion* to the shell they will support.

Now one is ready to begin to adorn the shell and base and to build up the overall design. This can be simple or complex, but whichever, great care must be taken.

First attempts should be simple, make only the uncomplicated designs to begin with, then progress to the difficult creations when you are practised in the handling of the glues and trimmings and the shell and lacquers.

16

A few base designs in wood

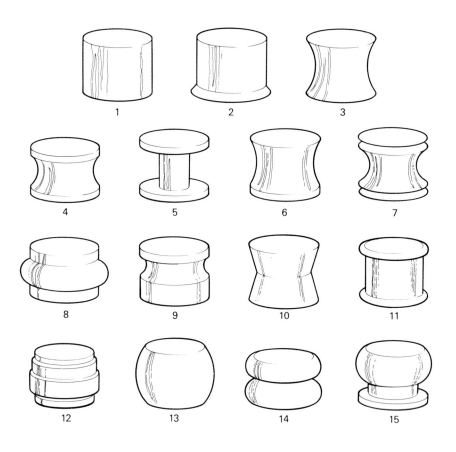

Figure 30

17
Colouring

Speed is all important to so many people these days, and in order to 'get things done' the aerosol spray-paint is resorted to. This is not only an effect-disaster, but denies any real craftsmanship or artistry. Use aerosol paints, even car spray paints, if you wish, but the aim of this book (I hope I don't sound pompous) is to advise on the use of only those materials that are as near to the lacquer and gold finish associated with antiques as possible. Embodied in the word 'antique' is the meaning 'long life'. The effort and time taken to make one of my egg designs is so great that only the finest materials are *worth* handling.

Of course these can be expensive and whilst I aim rather high now, I did start with more humble things.

Colouring the shell can be effected in many ways, either with watercolours or oil paints or acrylics, for instance, and these are most convenient. They must be applied to the shell with skill so as to avoid streaking or ridging, especially where the thicker acrylics are concerned.

Sandpaper the shell thoroughly first, removing every blemish, then take a knitting needle or a paint brush or some thin dowelling, push this through the holes made in the shell when it was blown, and in this way hold the shell and apply the colour evenly from one end to the other (Figure 31).

Allow each coat, of whatever colour material used, to dry for a day before applying the next. If the shell has been cut with the egg

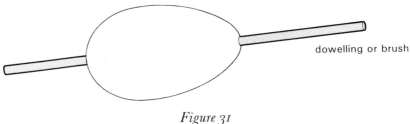

dowelling or brush

Figure 31

inside, then either colour the two halves, or the door and the egg-shell, before hingeing, but better, hinge first, glueing the hinge to the raw shell. This makes for a safer bond between the hinge and the shell.

This brings me to mentioning the finest, and again very convenient, form of colour. Acetate lacquer in the form of nail polish, or varnish, is available in many colours and it is supplied with a handy brush!

In the early 1970s one had a wide range of colours and I stocked up with greens of every hue and lovely blues and purples and oyster. Fashion changes, yet it repeats itself, and it is to be hoped some more colours will again become available other than the red-brown range.

This lacquer is difficult to apply and must be worked with quickly as it reacts to air and sets almost immediately. Using this lacquer it is better to cut the shell first, even blown stored ones, though I would always fix the hinge into position before lacquering. Speed here is important as one has to apply the lacquer very deftly.

The first coating is a disappointment as it shows the shell through, with any blemishes. This is to be expected and the second and third coat, too, show the shell through. To cover a shell successfully one needs to apply ten to fourteen coats of lacquer and allow a day between each coat for drying. This is a long process, yet the result is totally satisfying and quite beautiful. The lacquer colour sets with a deep glow and, when seen set off by other decoration such as gold roping or jewels, looks and lasts like the fired lacquers one finds on the brass-work of the East.

18

Trimmings

The best trimmings are those which are not associated with the obvious, those, for instance, which differ from lampshade trimming or cushion cording. Though these materials can be used and made to seem attractive, they always look what they are and are not really suitable for creating a decorative design which has the traditional feel of 'time past'.

Where, though, are alternatives to be found? It is a case of searching out trimming from old dresses, old curtain hems; using brocade pieces cut into strips, even using wool which, when stuck to the shell surface can be trimmed of hairy bits with scissors and covered with liquid gold leaf. There are many ways of achieving this traditional effect.

Gold cording can be obtained in a variety of sizes from some of the department stores or from Ells & Farrier (see 34, Suppliers), or, perhaps, from church furnishers who supply cording used for embroidering altar frontals and ecclesiastical robes.

The main point is that to decorate a shell which achieves what I call a 'traditional effect' (I mean in keeping with, say, the Fabergé style) only use those materials that are in sympathy with rococo or Empire or Commemorative designs. Try and avoid lampshade trimming and seek out the old pieces, often to be found in the charity shops – shoe buckles, hat flowers and ribbons, old silk and so forth. By using these old things you are adding to the 'treasure' of your egg.

19

Linings

The only thing to use is silk. Silk manages well, into the inside of either upper or lower halves of the shell. One can use other stuffs, such as georgette or crêpe, but whatever you use steer clear of any man-made fibre such as nylon. There is plenty of silk around and quite small quantities can be bought in delightful pale pastel shades at little expense. Of course, as I suggested in 'Trimmings', old silk can be found in charity shops – old lingerie or bits of dance dresses, for instance. As an alternative one can use lace, which must or should also be old and of a 'period', but really, silk is the best and it looks good.

To make a lining for the lid of a casket, first measure the circumference of the egg and then the average depth of the lid (Figure 32).

Then cut a length of material this size.

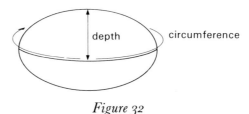

Figure 32

Now thread a needle with matching thread and sew a running stitch as indicated by the dotted line (Figure 33). Draw the material into a bunch and tie it off. The material now ruched up at one end

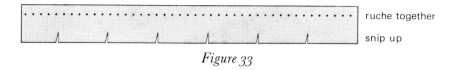

Figure 33

will spread out at the other and it will be seen that this can be 'managed' into the inside of the shell. Glue the ruched end so that it adheres to the roof of the lid and split several snips up into the 'skirt' of the lining, this way it will be easier to fit it snugly to the lower inside.

This is basic procedure for all linings.

20
Finials

Finials are the top decorating feature of a design, the adornment that sits on top of the lid of a casket or above an open door and tends to set off the whole design. It could be called the 'crowning glory', yet it need not be opulent. It must, though, be in keeping with the scheme as a whole and be in proportion to the overall size of the stand and egg-shell.

One can devise finials from a variety of different pieces, such as beads, large pearls or paste diamonds set in cord rings. When the time arrives to fit a finial, the design will suggest something appropriate from the 'findings' that have been collected. It may be a small silver crown or a single large bead of cut glass or a golden ball, etc.

Keeping proportion in mind, mark the actual centre of the top of the shell with a pencil. If the shell is lacquered then make a scratch mark with a needle. Now mix a small amount of Araldite Rapid and allow it to partly harden, then place a blob of the glue onto the scratch mark on the shell and place the finial into position. Turn the shell around to check that the finial is, in fact, positioned centrally.

It is fun collecting small items that are suitable for using as finials. Adapting unlikely things, on the other hand, is a challenge. For instance, the ornamental handle of a disused clock key, if sawn off the winding shaft, can make an attractive finial. From the sewing box again, a small silver thimble, the kind that used to be put in Christmas puddings, may be used. Small metal birds from hat decorations or ear-rings turned upside down are some other ideas.

As with trimmings and linings and jewels, be on the look-out wherever you are for these finials – on holiday is a good idea and searching for them can brighten a dull day.

21
Latching

To latch the front of a jewelled egg-shell is as about as necessary as putting a clasp on a prayer book. It is excess to requirements and a complication which, if the shell is opened too roughly, can cause breakage. Having said that, there are pretty latches that can be obtained and some people may like to add them to their design (see Figure 34).

Figure 34

These are three typical designs, where the top flap presses onto a stud fixed to the lower half of the shell. The problem is not only to make sure that the latch fits the stud slackly, so as to avoid having to press too hard to close it, but to shape what is a straight-backed hinged latch to the curved contour of the egg-shell.

They can look delightful if applied sensibly and are an apt finish to certain casket designs, but on the whole I tend to allow the weight of the upper half of the shell, with its decorations and trimming, to close any of the caskets I make.

The only latch that would seem to me to be appropriate would be one that locks, as one can find on many commercial wooden jewel boxes and for that matter on prayer books. The locking is the thing, making the item private exclusively to its owner. I have yet to find a locking latch that would be suitable for mounting into an egg-shell decoration.

22

Musical movements

Small musical movements, either made in Switzerland or Japan, can be obtained which, with ingenuity can be incorporated into an egg design (see 35, Suppliers).

I have found that the only really practical place to mount these musical movements is within the base. The egg-shell is too fragile to take the constant starting and stopping of the movement.

If you build up your own base, then you can make room for the movement when planning it, or if you turn your base on a lathe, from wood, then you must make the base hollow and be sure that the hollow is large enough to accommodate the movement.

Starting and stopping the movement is a problem but this can be solved by so placing a wire rod, which has been attached to a jewel that is a part of your design, that, on moving the jewel, the wire rod obstructs the fly-wheel of the movement, causing the tune to stop playing.

Provision must be made for the winding key, either by making a tiny pocket somewhere in the interior of your design or by leaving the key on the winding shaft, which will protrude from the bottom of the base, and mounting the base on legs. If you decide on the latter then remember the overall proportion of the *whole design*.

One idea of a musical egg is the surprise of the music and therefore concealing the switch is important. This is where your ingenuity comes in but with practice and thought many ways will occur to you. The fun is in inventing your own.

Here is a list of some of the tunes that are available and are most appropriate for inclusion in an egg design.

Anniversary Waltz.
Ave Maria.
Blue Danube.
Brahms's Lullaby.
Greensleeves.
Happy Birthday to You.
Some Enchanted Evening.
Westminster Chimes.
Bless This House.
Roses from the South.
Loch Lomond.
Waltz of the Flowers.
Wedding March.
Land of my Fathers.
When Irish Eyes are Smiling.
Sound of Music.
Yankee Doodle.
Oranges and Lemons.
Swan Lake.
Für Elise.
Silent Night.
Adeste Fideles.
Minuet (Boccherini).

If ordering from any supplier, always give an alternative in case a tune is out of stock.

23
Jewels: Real or artificial

Diamonds, emeralds, sapphires, rubies, pearls. Gold, platinum, silver. Amethyst, citrine, topaz, garnet, moonstone. Jade, agate, ivory, ebony, lapis luzuli.

These are some of the basic materials which are used in making precious jewellery or ornamental adornments and they are costly items indeed.

I am often asked why I do not use real jewels when making my eggs, but mounting any of them on something as fragile as a bird's egg would be risky, to say the least, especially for setting diamonds or sapphires, or if using minerals such as gold or silver.

Fortunately though, there are many good and honourable imitation stones and minerals that can be used. There is much historical evidence for the use of the artificial stone. Artificial glass jewels have been used by craftsmen for hundreds of years. As long ago as 1500 BC red, blue and green glass was used for personal adornments.

As early as the seventeenth century a method of making imitation pearls was invented in Paris. Small glass beads were made, the insides of which were hollow. A pearly lacquer, made from fish scales, was applied to the interior of the glass beads and when this was dry the inside was filled with molten wax to give them weight and make them hang well around the neck. Nowadays, imitation pearls are made from alabaster glass, a cloudy glass bead around which is coated lacquer made from sardine scales. The best artificial pearls are those which have been dipped in lacquer most times, sometimes as many as ten times, giving them a deep lustre and a long wearing life.

Semi-precious stones are not so expensive and can be used for special egg designs. They have to be set correctly, though, so that their brilliance shows to advantage. A faceted citrine, for instance, would need a setting made for it appropriate to the design of the egg-shell and the setting would need to be lined with silver foil so that the light would be reflected back through the cuts.

Garnets are easily available and not too expensive but they absorb light and would only look fine set upon a brilliant white, well lacquered egg-shell which would encourage light to shine through them.

Topaz comes in lovely shades of yellow and gold, brown and blue and there is a pale grey-fawn colour, called a smoky topaz. This last colour is set off beautifully against a pale rose or pale green lacquer.

Easiest of all to obtain and use are the masses of imitation jewels that are available and all of which are made of glass. Imitation rubies are made from glass to which has been added salts of gold or copper. The artificial stone is cut and backed with a mirroring finish or is covered in foil, for reflecting light. Rhinestones are made by melting fine rods of coloured glass, or even finer threads of different coloured glass, into a paste which is then fused together and afterwards cut into the many-hued brilliants seen sewn onto evening handbags or dresses.

Another imitation which gives the illusion of the real thing is the paste diamond. These are often moulded first and the facets then polished to a fine finish. As well as diamonds, these paste stones imitate rubies and sapphires and emeralds, any of the fine stones you can think of. (The word paste refers to the mixture of glass before firing.)

24
Jewels: Collecting and use

There are many ways of collecting jewels. One can buy them or beg them or one can find them by rummaging amongst junk stalls in markets. I am, of course, talking about imitation jewels, paste ones. To use the real thing would be excessively expensive, though I have often been asked to 'work with the real thing'. My reply is, 'Would you care for me to set expensive jewels on something as fragile as a goose's egg?' It is just not practical, except, perhaps as a commission for an eccentric, for a very rich person.

Buying can be expensive but is not so costly that it would put off an enthusiast spending for a special effect. Modern costume jewellery is ideal for this purpose. One can buy pendants or ropes of pearls or coloured jewelled necklaces, which by cutting up in various ways can be used to most attractive effect when decorating a shell.

Loose jewels can also be bought from most good handicraft shops. A word of warning, though, if buying the flat-backed cabochons, either round or oval. They will, if too large, be impossible to fit well to the convex surface of the egg-shell (see Figure 35 A). The only way round this problem is to devise a setting which merges with the surface. This can be made by building up a series of gold rope mountings *on the shell* and then setting the cabochon jewel within (see Figure 35 B).

Ropes of pearls of all sizes, ropes of paste diamonds and other coloured imitation stones can also be bought, as can separate, cut jewels. Only the finest of these should be used, especially if blending

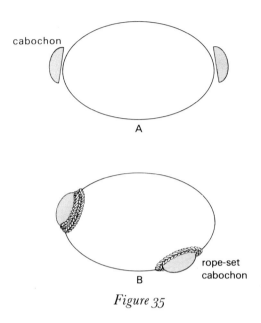

cabochon

A

rope-set
cabochon

B

Figure 35

in with the old, 'antique' ones, and plastic should be avoided at all costs.

Remember to look in drawers and cupboards, especially to ask your grandparents to search their's for you, they may have some 'long lost' treasures which will be fine to incorporate in a design. I am thinking of old cuff-links, tie-pins, badges, studs and brooches.

There are many places where jewels may be found and cut up and used again. Old dusty broken brooches, for instance, can be scrubbed with a toothbrush and soap and will sparkle anew ready for re-use.

Keep your eyes open when passing junk shops which have trays or boxes of old jewellery outside. So many brilliants can be found there and cost very little. The jewels can be taken out of broken settings and reset using gold cording. If you are to become an egg decoration enthusiast you must gather a large collection of this re-cyclable jewellery and have it around your working area where it can readily be seen. Just being able to see a quantity of colourful sparkling gems can inspire a whole creation.

Let me repeat, only use good stuff – good silk or antique lace for trimming the insides and good jewels. There are many such things lying around the charity shops and buying them helps the cause. Ask your friends if they have any bits they don't want and ask them to ask their friends. This way you are sure to come by some choice and unique pieces.

Do not throw anything away, you never know when you will be able to use even the smallest piece of adornment. Such a piece may 'save' or 'make' a design you are working on.

25

Decorating an egg-shell without jewels

You do not have to use jewels in order to enjoy and join in the art of decorating egg-shells. There are many ways of creating a pleasing effect using a variety of mediums. An advantage of most of these is that they can be worked on in front of the fire using a tray on the knee on which to put the materials.

Here are a few methods or ideas that I have tried and which seem to have worked, at least they have lasted over the years; by that I mean that the design has not faded or the effect diminished.

First, decorating the egg-shells whole, without first cutting them – indeed the intention is *not* to cut them but to decorate the shell whole after either blowing out the contents or after hard boiling the inside.

If blown, then before working on an egg-shell, make sure that its interior is quite dry. Either leave it in the sun for a week (optimistic in our climate), or put it on a shelf in the greenhouse or around the pilot lights on top of a gas cooker. The important thing is to dry out the interior and the shell so as to avoid any colour 'running' or spoiling because of moisture seeping through the shell's surface.

Prepare any shell first by sandpapering the surface as smooth as possible. This does two things: it cleans the shell thoroughly and it removes any extrusions or bumps, pieces of dirt or imperfect shell surface. If done correctly the surface of the egg-shell becomes as smooth as paper.

For all these ideas you will need to have to hand some kitchen paper, for wiping your hands of excess colouring or dirt or perspiration and sometimes for holding the egg-shell with in order to prevent grease from your hands penetrating it. All shells have a natural greasiness, it is their natural protective element against the weather. The sandpapering will remove most of this grease, but should a shell have too much grease and refuse to take colour, water colour for instance, then a coating of white emulsion paint or white vinyl paint will seal the shell surface.

Here are some ideas, the simple ones first.

Lead Pencil

Use an HB pencil and draw on the egg-shell. Think first about your pattern, it may be geometric, or a scene or some simple flowing outlines. Draw faintly at first and use only one half of the shell, call it the front. When the outline is complete, strengthen the lines, shading some areas or leaving the design open.

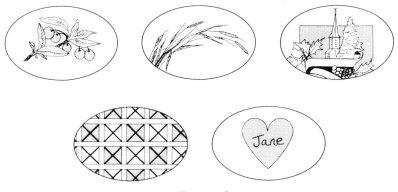

Figure 36

Figure 36 shows some designs that can be drawn with a pencil. Ball-point pens, too, can be used, as can felt-tipped pens, and this will bring colour into your designs. With all these attempts remember that a good design must have clarity.

These whole egg-shells, when decorated, look very attractive in

67

a bowl and cause a lot of comment from friends. Making them is a useful introduction to handling egg-shells and thinking about different effects.

Paints: acrylics, oils and water colours

Using paints can cause problems both of correct application and of accidental application! To prevent messy effects, again *think first, take care and be simple.*

Acrylic paints are convenient as they can be mixed with water for thinning and of course they intermix with each other. The white acrylic paint can be applied all over the egg-shell first as an undercoating, before painting. If you do this, then you must thin down the paint and apply even layers, allowing each to dry before overpainting. It will take three layers to coat a shell satisfactorily. If you paint an all-over 'base' colour before commencing your design and use the paint too thickly, it will streak and dry in ridges or in brush-marks and all the sandpapering in the world will not remove these marks, so mix the base colour first to a milky consistency, then cover the egg-shell.

Miniature painting is an art that needs years of practice, so unless you are an experienced artist, or just a 'natural' one whose hidden or latent talent is coming out, start off with simple effects, getting used to brush-work and to the feel of the paint.

Figure 37 shows some suggestions to set you thinking.

match-stick people can be amusing

large flower drawings

blocks of colour

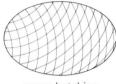

cross-hatching

blobs of colour

Figure 37

Plain gilding

Using gold leaf is very expensive and fraught with difficulties, mainly because the leaf is so finely beaten that it blows away easily, or falls onto the work unevenly and therefore wastefully. There can be more waste than use, which is regrettable as there is no other gold effect quite like the real thing.

Fortunately there are gilding alternatives available and with them a reasonably convincing gold finish can be achieved; again this is a tray-top hobby.

Bottles of gold paint come either water-based or with spirit and oil added. The latter are the best as there is no danger of them being repulsed by the natural grease in the egg-shell. No matter how careful one is, some grease will be on the egg-shell, if only from your own fingers or palm.

The gold comes in different colours. Antique Gold, though so called, comes in a variety of shades depending on the manufacturer. Some are very sickly and pale whilst others are too coppery, though all bear the same term, 'Antique Gold', on the label.

A reliable source for good gold paint is a picture-framing shop. There does seem to be a standard of gold colour that is used for picture framing and this gold paint is sold by reputable framing shops.

One that I would recommend is made by Robersons of London and is called 'Ormoline'. Their 'Deep Gold' is most satisfying and their other 'golds' are equally good. You must buy thinner at the same time as this gold paint applies better if thinned down by mixing a little in the pot lid with thinner and then painting. Winsor and Newton make a metallic 'bronze', really a contradiction as it is gold and quite a good one. The paint number is 610 and is sold in small flat-topped pots labelled 'Poster Paint'. Reeves Poster Colour includes an 'Imitation Gold', number 75, though this is much lighter in colour, more like 14-carat gold. Rowney do an even lighter 'Imitation Gold'. You must look around and decide which you prefer; or use them all.

Whichever appeals to you, coat the whole shell with three coats, leaving each coat to dry. A display of different coloured gold eggs looks good anywhere. It is easy too.

A variation using plain gold is to scratch a design through the gold, revealing the shell. Another variation is painting a pattern over the gold.

These gold eggs are very attractive either singly or in groups and are certain winners for bazaars or for church fêtes.

Cover all painted egg-shells with clear lacquer – this preserves them and imparts a really fine finish, especially to the gold ones. Use clear nail varnish.

Indian ink

Indian ink is very good for silhouettes and also for fine precise drawing. When using a pen for drawing, the egg-shell must first be sandpapered very finely as any irregularities or slight bumps on the shell will upset the flow of the pen's nib and will ruin your work.

Using Indian ink as a medium, 'Musical Signatures' can be fun to make and give. You need to know about musical notation, but this is not very difficult to grasp, in fact all you need to remember is E, G, B, D, F, A, C.

A name may be Brian Frederick Ashton. This would give the initials B.F.A. and in musical notation, on the treble clef, would look like Figure 38.

Figure 38

To look more interesting, you can double up the notes and add a key and time signature (Figure 39). This is meaningless musically, but on an egg-shell it can represent an original gift.

Figure 39

Actual musical quotations can be used, easy ones such as *Ba Ba Black Sheep*, or *After the Ball*. A musical enthusiast could run the five-line stave around the egg-shell as a spiral continuing band and write music on it – *Happy Birthday to You*, for instance – and then sign it.

Figure 40

26

Découpage

Briefly this is a method of sinking a cut-out on to the egg-shell, using many layers of lacquer, so that it becomes a part of the surface.

The advantage of découpage is that if one can't paint, then items such as parts of colour illustrations, carefully cut out, can be used as a substitute.

The field of material suitable for cutting for découpage is infinite. Magazines, post cards, books, advertisements, wine bottle labels and cigar box interiors are just some of the sources. The latter, the cigar boxes, yield some pretty attractive miniature pictures, gold crowns and bows and flounces, and are useful in themselves for storing things.

Other than gold cut-outs that are available from craft shops, I am particular in using those that are authentically antique and of the period, eighteenth-century prints for instance. There are many of these, humble and unimportant ones depicting a lovers' quarrel perhaps, or a trophy of flowers, that have no actual antique value, and are therefore reasonably priced, yet when cut and découpaged, look delightful. Victorian scraps too can be useful but they are often printed on thick paper and need sanding down to a thinness suitable for laying on the curve of the shell. These depict ferns, cupids and angels, small scenes, hands and faces, etc.

If the cut-out to be découpaged is too thick, as I have said it can be sandpapered thinner. Often, though, the back paper can be peeled off, it may be off an old photo or a cut-out from a picture post card. Don't forget that the shell surface is convex and in order to 'manage' the découpage cut-out to adhere well to the surface of the shell, small snips should be made around its edges. These then 'bind' together and the cut-out blends easily with the shape of the shell.

To prevent the colour running when over-lacquering a piece of découpage work it should first of all be sealed, either using découpage sealer, available at craft shops, or acrylic medium. A sealer should always be used if applying stipple-engraved prints as the paper on which the printing was originally done is very porous and lacquer applied directly onto this paper will soak in and make a mess of the print, sometimes obliterating the delicate original. If an 'antique' finish is desired, then use a yellow-tinted lacquer *only* over the surface of the découpage.

Découpage is not a quick method of decoration. To be effective the result should look and feel to be a part of the shell. This means applying many layers of final lacquer to achieve a really good depth, sometimes as many as fourteen coats, allowing each twenty-four hours in which to dry. This process is lengthy but rewarding, and will serve as an illustration of just how much time is taken in making a really excellent decorated egg.

27

Dried flowers, grasses and 'things'

These are most useful for decorating the inside of shell designs and are easily obtainable. Dried flowers and grasses speak for themselves, but 'things' is left to your imagination.

If one does have a garden, or even access to one, then the things that can be found there are many and variable. Flowers of any sort can be dried simply by hanging upside down in bunches in a warm place and so many keep their colour. If this way of collecting is impossible for you (yet who cannot organise a window-box?) then most florist's shops sell dried flowers and grasses. One only needs a few varieties to fill a few shells.

The countryside at all times is a marvellous place to pick and collect specimens, steering clear of the protected ones. Winter is an especially rewarding time of the year as then there are so many heads and seed pods available. One can, for instance, collect a few ears of wheat and, after separating the ears, gild them and arrange them in delightful ways.

The garden from June onwards has any amount of material just waiting. Geraniums, for example. When cutting off the dead heads, save them and hang them upside down. The petals will retain their brilliant and many-coloured hues and look fine inside a shell. Anchusa is a lovely blue, as are all the small petals of the cornflower. The seed heads of Love-in-the-Mist are fantastic and the soft curls of clematis seed heads look fine inside a shell, perhaps with a bird sitting on them as though on a nest.

'Things' means all the little stones found in garden soil that, when washed, look quite different, small pieces of broken pottery or crockery, pieces of worn glass found in all colours on the beach, shells, lichen, bark; there are so many, and all can help in creating a design.

28
Perfume and pot pourri in eggs

A charming way to fill the lower interior of an egg-shell is by hiding pot pourri underneath a decorative cover. The result will be fragrant for many years to come and the perfume can always be reactivated by the addition of more perfume. You can also ring the changes and alter the scent.

A very simple pot pourri can be made using only lavender flowers. These can be bought in sachets but it is more interesting to make your own collection of flower heads. If you have none in your garden, you are sure to have a friend who will let you pick a few spikes, and you only need a few. They must be picked when the flowers are just coming into bloom. Dry the spikes well first, then strip the flowers off the spike and keep them in an air-tight bag until you are ready to use them. If the scent needs activating, then brighten it with a dash of lavender water or lavender oil.

There are many other pot pourris that can be bought such as English Garden or Elizabethan. These are ready preserved and mixed and are not very expensive, especially as only a little is used in each egg-shell.

It is more fun to make your own pot pourri and it is easy, more so if you have a garden. Save the petals of any flowers, though the base petal of all mixed pot pourri is from the rose. Varieties such as Fragrant Cloud or Zephrin Drouhin have a wonderful smell but there are many others easily accessible to everyone. Sweet pea, marigold, carnation, lilac and mock orange are also good and look colourful. All petals will keep their colour if dried quickly and the best way of doing this is to dry them in the sunshine, preferably in the greenhouse so that the wind will not blow them around.

When the petals are quite dry mix them well together, put some lavender flowers in if you wish. Then, add a small amount (half a teaspoon to a cup of flowers) of powdered orris root. This keeps in the natural oils that are in the petals and preserves their scent and their combined perfume will last longer. Orris root powder is easily obtained from 'alternative' shops, or from herb shops. Essential oils such as bergamot or lavender, rose, lily of the valley and many others can also be bought from these shops.

If obtaining pot pourri or making pot pourri is beyond you, then there are alternatives. Use a wad of cotton wool as a 'soak' for your perfume, or tissue paper or blotting paper torn into tiny pieces, fill the lower half of your egg-shell with them and saturate them with flower oil or toilet water, even after-shave lotion!

I like to think my designs will be permanent and long-lasting so I only use oils and perfumes from Floris of Jermyn Street in London, but there are many other ways of perfuming your design – the more exotic bath essences, for instance.

After you have decided on your filling, this must be protected by a cover. A piece of stiff cardboard, cut to the circumference of the egg-shell and punched with holes is a good cover. Cut the cardboard so that it fits about 1cm below the rim of the egg-shell to allow for interior decoration. Now glue the cardboard into place *after* putting in your filling material, pot pourri or cotton wool, etc.

To make the interior attractive, cover the cardboard with suitable material and then arrange artificial or dried flowers into a bouquet or pattern, edging the shell with gold roping or beads, anything that happens to suggest itself from amongst your 'findings'.

Another way of adding perfume to an egg-shell design is to add the pot pourri or filling material into the actual base on which the egg and stand are set. If you build your own base it will be easy to organise a space or cavity to hold your perfume material. An advantage of this is that it leaves the egg-shell empty and ready for containing a surprise, or for use as a jewel casket. A perfumed base will also add to the attraction of a design which has a door-opening. Inside may be a scene of the countryside or a figurine and one can relate these to a particular perfume. With figures, rose oil goes very well and with scenes of the countryside the 'greener' scents are better, lime, lemon or geranium, perhaps mixed.

There are so many ways of completing a perfumed egg-shell design and I hope some of the things I have mentioned will stimulate your imagination and you will create and invent many original ways. It is always a joy to open an egg and smell again a fragrance that you may have 'trapped' within.

A last thought – don't forget violets. There are some very attractive artificial ones that can be bought, or better still, found as trimmings on old hats, and violet perfume and oil is long-lasting and, just by the way, is an old herbal cure for a headache.

29
Ideas for anniversaries

Birthstones have been worn as lucky charms throughout the centuries. It is thought that the attributes of the stone are imparted to the wearer and some people carry with them, either as a ring or hanging around the neck, or just in the pocket, one stone of each month of the year, just to be sure to absorb as much as possible from them. These people may be rare, but most at some time or another think about the relevance of jewellery and the suitability of certain stones for, say, a birth date. Here is a list of stones for each month.

January	Garnet.
February	Amethyst.
March	Aquamarine, bloodstone or jasper.
April	Diamond or rock crystal.
May	Emerald, agate or chrysoprase.
June	Pearls, moonstone or alexandrite.
July	Ruby or cornelian.
August	Peridot, sardonyx or jade.
September	Sapphire, lapis lazuli or coral.
October	Opal, tourmaline or rose sapphire.
November	Topaz, amber or citrine.
December	Turquoise or blue zircon.

Here are some symbolic meanings of precious and semi-precious stones.

Agate   This is helpful for prosperity and it protects against danger.

Alexandrite   This changes colour, sometimes it is blue or amethyst or greenish, and is said to contain all the virtues of the sapphire, emerald and amethyst.

Coral   This imparts wisdom and reason and it wards off fear and temptation to violence.

Diamond   Diamonds bring peace and serenity, also constancy, fidelity and innocence, hence its popularity as a wedding stone.

Emerald   This enhances love and brings strength to old age. It brings popularity to those who wear one.

Garnet   Constancy is foremost, then friendliness and charity.

Jade   A symbol of immortality. Has curative powers and wards off disagreeable dreams. In past centuries in India, only men of the highest moral character were permitted to wear jade. In China it is sacred.

Jet   Symbolises grief and sadness but will also ward off apparitions or mental fear.

Moonstone   A symbol of purity and chastity.

Onyx   The onyx symbolises fear and sadness. Whilst it promotes chastity it induces quarrels and ominous forebodings.

Opal   Unlucky for all except those born in October, it is said. Originally attributed to give wealth and power to its owner. If it is unlucky for the wearer it will become dull. Milky-looking opals bring on sadness and melancholia.

Pearl   Symbolises tears, both of sadness and gladness; also patience and purity and faithfulness.

Ruby   Loyalty, charity and courage, but when it seems deepest red, imbues boldness and anger or cruelty.

Topaz Gives idyllic love, imbues faithfulness and sobriety. It appeases anger and turns sadness into happiness.

Sapphire The sapphire brings peace and calm to the wearer. It symbolises justice, loyalty and truth.

Precious stones and metals have, throughout time, come to be associated with anniversaries. There are the gold and silver weddings, for example. The following is a list of stones and names for weddings.

1 Rose wedding, beryl wedding, or paper wedding.
2 Crystal wedding or cotton wedding.
3 Chrysoprase wedding or leather wedding.
4 Moonstone wedding or silk wedding.
5 Cornelian wedding or wood wedding.
6 Peridot wedding or sugar wedding.
7 Coral wedding or wool wedding.
8 Opal wedding or clay wedding.
9 Citrine wedding or willow wedding.
10 Turquoise wedding or tin wedding.
11 Garnet wedding.
12 Amethyst wedding or linen wedding.
13 Agate wedding.
14 Ivory wedding or lace wedding.
15 Topaz wedding.
20 China wedding.
25 Silver wedding.
30 Pearl wedding.
35 Jade wedding.
40 Ruby wedding.
45 Sapphire wedding.
50 Golden wedding.
60 Diamond wedding.

Wedding anniversaries can be brought good fortune if a person receives a gift containing a suggestion of the jewel appropriate for the occasion; why not a decorated egg?

Flowers too have their place in egg-shell decoration. Either they can make an attractive display inside the shell or they can be applied to the outside and covered in lacquer for protection.

Flowers that bring luck for the month of birth are as follows:

January	Carnation or Snowdrop.
February	Primrose.
March	Daffodil.
April	Daisy.
May	Lilly of the valley.
June	Rose.
July	Water lily.
August	Gladiolus.
September	Aster.
October	Dahlia.
November	Chrysanthemum.
December	Holly.

Certain flowers have qualities associated with them just as do jewels. They are often worn or chosen for giving to express a certain sentiment.

The most popular ones are:

Carnation	Fidelity, trust, virtue.
Daisy	Humility.
Forget-me-not	Remembrance.
Honeysuckle	Constancy.
Hyacinth	Friendship.
Lily	Steadfastness.
Marigold	Wisdom.
Pansy	Good will.
Poppy	Faithfulness.

Rose (red)	Nobility.
Rose (white)	Valour and bravery.
Rose (yellow)	Infidelity.
Rosemary	Love and tears.
Violet	Patience and hope.

From these lists, it will be seen that there are many computations possible for anniversary eggs.

You may make an egg for a fourth wedding anniversary that took place in February. This would need moonstones and silk and amethysts and primroses.

The egg could be a pale primrose colour, trimmed with gold and set on a gold or gilded stand, itself set on a black base similar to a cup-stand. The inside would be lined with heliotrope silk and contain a surprise, say a small bouquet of artificial primroses. The shell would be adorned with ropes of set artificial amethysts and the finial would be a (real) moonstone.

A husband and wife team, or one or the other, could plan and make a suitable egg for each of their anniversaries, keeping them in a glass cabinet so as to show them off.

The variations are obviously endless and I hope these lists will be stimulating.

30
Colours and their meanings

When creating a design for an egg-shell, its stand and its base, colour consideration can be more important than may at first appear.

It is simple to decide to make, say, a green design, or a silver or white design, or one that is 'all gold and diamonds', but colours have their own innate meanings and by understanding a little about the virtues, or otherwise, of colours, their use can be the deciding factor of a design. Understanding the various meanings of any one colour can help in achieving overall harmony.

The reason for using a particular colour can often stimulate a whole design and set you thinking about effects that would not readily have come to mind, and this is especially so when blending or mixing colours, as their characteristics are also involved.

Just as jewels have their own meaning, so do colours. Here is a list of them.

Red (Pink, Carmine, Crimson, Rose)
Red is associated with passion, with sexual excitement; with anger and with birth, creation. Rose shades mean a dream, a fancy or an illusion.

Yellow (Topaz, Lemon, Primrose, Saffron)
Oriental associations. Yellow means eternality, it is an outgoing colour. Variations in shades will vary these meanings. Saffron is used spiritually.

Orange (Ginger, Peach, Bronze, Ochre)
These are powerful colours and carry a mixture of the meanings of both red and yellow. Orange and its hues denotes occult power and mystery.

Blue (Azure, Turquoise, Indigo, Aquamarine)
Blue is a colour associated with heaven, with the sky and all things celestial. It is also an intellectual colour and it, too, means fidelity. Dark blue means depth of feeling.

Green (Jade, Emerald, Adam, Lime)
A colour of nature, represents life and vigour, also jealousy. A colour of classicism, of design simplicity. When mixed with blue has meanings of the sea.

White (Ivory, Pearl, Chalk, Marble)
The colour of innocence. A very feminine colour, especially if used with silver, hence wedding cakes. When combined with gold has associations with royalty.

Silver (White, Grey, Ash, Lead)
Another aspect of innocence. Is connected with the moon, with light and with knowledge. White is extremely feminine.

Gold (Copper, Citrine, Gilt, Gamboge)
The colour of the sun. Represents both power and mystery. Is strongly associated with truth and is essentially masculine. Majesterial and royal.

The following colours should be avoided unless a special effect is aimed at, bearing in mind their meanings.

Black (Ink, Ebony, Japan, Jet)
Black is the colour of death. It has associations with gloom and distress. It embodies secretiveness and is the colour of the devil.

Purple (Gentian, Violet, Mauve, Amethyst)
These colours are very strong and will dominate a design. Purple holds power and embraces mystery. Only to be used with caution.

Lilac (Heliotrope, Lavender, Puce, Mulberry)
These are shades associated with death. They are also connected with age, with times that are past.

Brown (Chestnut, Cinnamon, Maroon, Coffee)
All are earthy colours and need great care if being used. They can be sensational and daring. Browns are the colours of hiding and of secretiveness.

There are many other variations of all these colours but the basic attributes are always the same. It may be useful to refer to this list when thinking about a design.

In any case, it is fun to know about colours and their associations and this knowledge will add to the attraction of egg-shell decoration. Whatever the colour used, beware of muddy effects; once again it is clarity that counts and careless use of colour can spoil a whole design.

31
Surprises

Opening a decorated egg and finding something within, say a bouquet of flowers in a beautiful setting of silk and smelling of fragrant perfume, is a surprise in itself.

To make sure your design is such that a surprise *is* a surprise, try and conceal any opening by making it a part of the design and thereby impossible to detect. This is not possible with a drawer, but with an opening door or a lifting hinged lid of a jewel casket, careful design can conceal the actual place of opening.

Once open, be it a door or a lid, the inside alone will be a surprise, but it must be in keeping with the overall design, in keeping with either the period or the 'feel' of the creation. It would be a poor surprise if, on opening a beautifully decorated baroque egg, inside there was a Scottie dog looking winsomely at you. More appropriate would be a small bisque cherub, perhaps sitting in a bower of dried moss. The Scottie dog would be more appropriate set in an egg designed with ferns and a scene of Scotland, or the countryside, applied by the découpage method.

There is no end to creating surprises, only to the patience and time needed to make them. The design in Figure 41 will show what *could* be done, though it is needlessly complicated.

When dreaming up complicated designs, it is as well to remember that halfway through making a creation, say after three weeks' work, the shell might split on you, or you will accidentally drop it or press too hard and split the lacquer.

These are surprises no one wants, but it is better to be warned; they do happen.

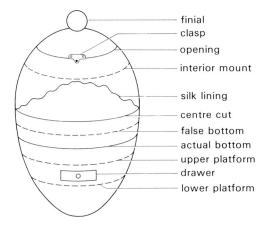

Figure 41

32
A list of various eggs

Ostrich
Emu
Rhea
Goose
Peacock
Pheasant
Turkey
Pigeon
Quail
Parakeet
Finch   and some exotic ones,

Cassowary
Pee-wee
Pharaoh Quail
Oriental Pheasant
Mandarin Duck
Mallard Duck
Bobwhite Quail
Aracauna
Banty
Zebra Finch

The above can be bought from egg suppliers. Many wild birds' eggs are protected by law but in America special breeders of wild birds have *infertile* eggs which they make available. It is these which are obtainable.

33

Costing decorated eggs for sale

First of all add up the cost of all the items you have used to make the decorated egg, including the egg itself. This last item can be more money than you would expect. Goose eggs, for example, are sometimes very expensive and it goes without saying that the larger ones, such as the rhea, the emu, or the ostrich will be expensive. Sometimes one has to buy twenty goose eggs to get only six that are really large enough for cutting and decorating. This means that you are left with several of differing sizes, some of which are of no use other than to paint for fun.

Add to the cost of the egg the cost of the trimming used, the surprise inside, the finial and the jewels used around the shell, the base and the stand and the baize with which the bottom of the stand is covered, everything, in fact, that you have used in the making of your decorated egg.

Now there is the time taken. Some egg designs take longer than others but none of the larger ones I make take less than thirty hours of careful work and thought. Time costs money and you must cost this into a price.

You cannot sell anything without some wrapping and a decorated egg needs not only protection, but something worthy of it. This is best arrived at by having boxes made. I have black patent boxes on which there is an ornamental label and I sign this and put inside a personal card. Don't forget tissue paper.

Add all these things together and you will arrive at your *cost*.

Now ask yourself what profit you need. You have to buy more material, etc., and this is where profits go.

If you are thinking of selling eggs on a regular basis, then you will have to have some sort of publicity. Easiest is having a card printed which you can give to people interested, or insert in window advertising. It is better to try and word the card in a timeless way and then have a quantity printed that will last you some time.

Should you be fortunate enough to have orders it may be necessary to post eggs off to clients. Packing will be needed and there will be the postage.

All in all, there are quite a lot of things to remember when thinking about how to arrive at a price for a decorated egg and I have not included phone calls and letters.

To a prospective buyer who might read this it may seem that all decorated eggs are wildly expensive. This need not be so, but obviously the more complicated the design, the more it will cost. However, really fine ones are heirlooms and – who knows? – may become the antiques of the future.

Although it is useful to have a guide as to how to price a decorated egg for sale, most people who make them will do them because they enjoy the hobby. The really big ones take so long to make that to cost them realistically would make them unsaleable.

34
Signing and photographing the egg

There will be many people who admire your work and ask if they can have one of your eggs. You may either sell them or give them away as presents. However they leave you, you should sign your work and have a photograph taken of each egg.

Sign the lacquered shell by using a fine brush dipped into gold paint and either use your name or initials. When this is dry, over-lacquer the signature – this will protect it. Some of your designs you can date. You would be surprised how time flies and you forget just when you did make a particular egg. You can use Indian ink for signing plain shells, or a hard finely sharpened pencil or a ball-point pen, anything that will make a mark, but try and make what you use in keeping with your design and always over-lacquer it.

Photograph *all* the eggs you make, even if only for a hobby. It is interesting to show them on a screen through a projector, though beware – this enlargement will show up any faults in your crafts-manship. Black and white or colour prints are most useful for later reference and for showing to people when you do not have an egg handy, or for remembering ones that you have made long after they have gone out of your possession.

35
Suppliers

Ells & Farrier, 5 Princes Street, Hanover Square, London.	Pearls, sequins, jewels, gold roping, beads of all kinds.
Coronet Trading Co., 44 Station Lane, Hornchurch, Essex.	Egg stands.
Happy Pastime, 27 Duke Street, Brighton, Sussex.	Flat-backed jewels, egg stands.
Southern Handicrafts, 25 Kensington Gardens, Brighton, Sussex.	Paste diamonds, musical movements, jewels, pearls.

Culpeper Ltd,
Hadstock House,
Linton, Cambridge.
Branches at
  London
  Bath
  Brighton
  Cambridge
	Herbs, spices, pot pourri, oils and
	perfumed waters, seeds and
	leaves, pomander scents, colognes;
	send return postage for
	catalogue.

Dorking
Guildford
Norwich
Salisbury
Winchester

Tradition,   Miniature models.
188 Piccadilly,   01 - 493 7452 NN
London.

Liberty & Co.,   Silks.
Regent Street,
London.

Hobbys   Musical movements.
109 Norwood High Street,   01 - 734 8393 NN
London.

Egg Elegance,   Write for catalogue; send SAE.
30 Red House Lane,
Bexleyheath, Kent.

Cotswold Crafts   Wide variety of egg decorating
Dept PC5   materials; write for catalogue; send
5 Whitehall,   SAE.
Stroud, Glos.

Egg Creations,   Catalogue 50p plus 14p postage.
160 Lower Higham Road,
Gravesend, Kent.

Kevajo Handicrafts,   Large range of accessories, eggs,
25 Sackville Road,   jewels, stands, etc.; catalogue plus
Bexhill-on-Sea,   postage.
East Sussex.

Silvia Cresswell, Mottram Road, Alderley Edge, Cheshire.	American findings.
Inheritance, 51 Wellesley Road, Great Yarmouth, Norfolk.	Goose egg-shells, quail, duck and turkey; minimum order 6. Egg kits, materials and instructions.
'Eggelegance'.	Same as Egg Elegance.
Egg Creations, 165/7 Church Street, Cliffe, Rochester, Kent.	

Suppliers overseas

Taylor House, corner of Bench & Perry Streets, Galena, Illinois, USA.	Jewels, roping, models, stands and bases.
National Artcraft Supply Co. 12213 Euclid Avenue, Cleveland, Ohio, USA.	Musical movements (Swiss and Japanese).
Schlitz, Goose Hatchery, Bancroft, Iowa, USA.	Goose eggs shipped anywhere.

To start off, find out your local handicraft supplier and the range there that is available. You may not have to seek far for most of the things you want. The above addresses are proved by myself. Ordering from the USA needs dollar exchange, find out the company's payment policy before ordering.

For further information about where to obtain supplies in America, what magazines are available on this hobby, write to:

Mrs Kit Stansbury,
Treasure Chest,
The Stansburys,
42 Colby Place,
Phillipsburg,
New Jersey,
USA.

36

Some materials

Items available from suppliers include such things as those listed below. This list is by no means exhaustive, but it shows a sample of the materials that are now available. The complete catalogues available from the suppliers are fascinating and well worth studying and poring over. An impressive selection of items suitable for individual tastes in design may be obtained. I would advise beginners, especially, to go steady at first in ordering materials. The temptation is to buy all and sundry without actually 'seeing' the use for some of the things and one can land up with a lot of decorating material that never gets used, yet has cost money! Here is the list:

Bases
Figures
Group figures
Finishes, such as gold leaf and colours
Clear gloss seals which dry like glass
Glues
Brushes
Egg-blowing equipment
Earrings
Corsage pins
Braids and cords
Gold chain
Pearls

Tiffany-set jewels
Marking pens
Battery operated turntables
Power drills
Beads of all sorts
Hinges

The list of materials is endless and fascinating, as the catalogues show.

37

The Egg Crafters Guild of Great Britain

A society for the advancement of egg decorating.

This was founded in 1979 by Joan Cutts and its aims are as follows:

> To promote and encourage the Craft of Egg Decoration.
> To exchange information.
> To seek to exert a progressive influence on standards of workmanship and design in Egg Craft.

For details of membership of the Guild, write to:

> Joan Cutts,
> The Studio,
> 7 Hylton Terrace,
> North Shields,
> Tyne and Wear.

A list of Area Representatives can be obtained, all of whom will be pleased to receive queries and information from egg decorators in their area.

Information will also be given about Egg Fayres and Egg Conventions that are to be held and members will receive a quarterly bulletin which contains up-to-date information, news and gossip covering all the activities connected with egg decorating.

Index